Paradise Regained

by John Milton

I, WHO erewhile the happy Garden sung

By one man's disobedience lost, now sing

Recovered Paradise to all mankind,

By one man's firm obedience fully tried

Through all temptation, and the Tempter foiled

In all his wiles, defeated and repulsed,

And Eden raised in the waste Wilderness.

Thou Spirit, who led'st this glorious Eremite

Into the desert, his victorious field

Against the spiritual foe, and brought'st him thence 10 By proof the undoubted Son of God, inspire,

As thou art wont, my prompted song, else mute,

And bear through highth or depth of Nature's bounds,

With prosperous wing full summed, to tell of deeds

Above heroic, though in secret done,

And unrecorded left through many an age:

Worthy to have not remained so long unsung.

Now had the great Proclaimer, with a voice

More awful than the sound of trumpet, cried .

Repentance, and Heaven's kingdom nigh at hand 20 To all baptized. To his great baptism flocked

With awe the regions round, and with them came

From Nazareth the son of Joseph deemed

To the flood Jordan--came as then obscure,

Unmarked, unknown. But him the Baptist soon

Descried, divinely warned, and witness bore

As to his worthier, and would have resigned

To him his heavenly office. Nor was long

His witness unconfirmed: on him baptized

Heaven opened, and in likeness of a Dove 30 The Spirit descended, while the Father's voice

From Heaven pronounced him his beloved Son.

That heard the Adversary, who, roving still

About the world, at that assembly famed

Would not be last, and, with the voice divine

Nigh thunder-struck, the exalted man to whom

Such high attest was given a while surveyed

With wonder; then, with envy fraught and rage,

Flies to his place, nor rests, but in mid air

To council summons all his mighty Peers, 40 Within thick clouds and dark tenfold involved,

A gloomy consistory; and them amidst,

With looks aghast and sad, he thus bespake:--

"O ancient Powers of Air and this wide World

(For much more willingly I mention Air,

This our old conquest, than remember Hell,

Our hated habitation), well ye know

How many ages, as the years of men,

This Universe we have possessed, and ruled

In manner at our will the affairs of Earth, 50 Since Adam and his facile consort Eve

Lost Paradise, deceived by me, though since

With dread attending when that fatal wound

Shall be inflicted by the seed of Eve

Upon my head. Long the decrees of Heaven

Delay, for longest time to Him is short;

And now, too soon for us, the circling hours

This dreaded time have compassed, wherein we

Must bide the stroke of that long-threatened wound

(At least, if so we can, and by the head 60 Broken be not intended all our power

To be infringed, our freedom and our being

In this fair empire won of Earth and Air)--

For this ill news I bring: The Woman's Seed,

Destined to this, is late of woman born.

His birth to our just fear gave no small cause;

But his growth now to youth's full flower, displaying

All virtue, grace and wisdom to achieve

Things highest, greatest, multiplies my fear.

Before him a great Prophet, to proclaim 70 His coming, is sent harbinger, who all

Invites, and in the consecrated stream

Pretends to wash off sin, and fit them so

Purified to receive him pure, or rather

To do him honour as their King. All come,

And he himself among them was baptized--

Not thence to be more pure, but to receive

The testimony of Heaven, that who he is

Thenceforth the nations may not doubt. I saw

The Prophet do him reverence; on him, rising 80 Out of the water, Heaven above the clouds

Unfold her crystal doors; thence on his head

A perfet Dove descend (whate'er it meant);

And out of Heaven the sovraign voice I heard,

'This is my Son beloved,--in him am pleased.'

His mother, than, is mortal, but his Sire

He who obtains the monarchy of Heaven;

And what will He not do to advance his Son?

His first-begot we know, and sore have felt,

When his fierce thunder drove us to the Deep; 90 Who this is we must learn, for Man he seems

In all his lineaments, though in his face

The glimpses of his Father's glory shine.

Ye see our danger on the utmost edge

Of hazard, which admits no long debate,

But must with something sudden be opposed

(Not force, but well-couched fraud, well-woven snares),

Ere in the head of nations he appear,

Their king, their leader, and supreme on Earth.

I, when no other durst, sole undertook 100 The dismal expedition to find out

And ruin Adam, and the exploit performed

Successfully: a calmer voyage now

Will waft me; and the way found prosperous once

Induces best to hope of like success."

He ended, and his words impression left

Of much amazement to the infernal crew,

Distracted and surprised with deep dismay

At these sad tidings. But no time was then

For long indulgence to their fears or grief: 110 Unanimous they all commit the care

And management of this man enterprise

To him, their great Dictator, whose attempt

At first against mankind so well had thrived

In Adam's overthrow, and led their march

From Hell's deep-vaulted den to dwell in light,

Regents, and potentates, and kings, yea gods,

Of many a pleasant realm and province wide.

So to the coast of Jordan he directs

His easy steps, girded with snaky wiles, 120 Where he might likeliest find this new-declared,

This man of men, attested Son of God,

Temptation and all guile on him to try--

So to subvert whom he suspected raised

To end his reign on Earth so long enjoyed:

But, contrary, unweeting he fulfilled

The purposed counsel, pre-ordained and fixed,

Of the Most High, who, in full frequence bright

Of Angels, thus to Gabriel smiling spake:--

"Gabriel, this day, by proof, thou shalt behold, 130 Thou and all Angels conversant on Earth

With Man or men's affairs, how I begin

To verify that solemn message late,

On which I sent thee to the Virgin pure

In Galilee, that she should bear a son,

Great in renown, and called the Son of God.

Then told'st her, doubting how these things could be

To her a virgin, that on her should come

The Holy Ghost, and the power of the Highest

O'ershadow her. This Man, born and now upgrown, 140 To shew him worthy of his birth divine

And high prediction, henceforth I expose

To Satan; let him tempt, and now assay

His utmost subtlety, because he boasts

And vaunts of his great cunning to the throng

Of his Apostasy. He might have learnt

Less overweening, since he failed in Job,

Whose constant perseverance overcame

Whate'er his cruel malice could invent.

He now shall know I can produce a man, 150 Of female seed, far abler to resist

All his solicitations, and at length

All his vast force, and drive him back to Hell--

Winning by conquest what the first man lost

By fallacy surprised. But first I mean

To exercise him in the Wilderness;

There he shall first lay down the rudiments

Of his great warfare, ere I send him forth

To conquer Sin and Death, the two grand foes.

By humiliation and strong sufferance 160 His weakness shall o'ercome Satanic strength,

And all the world, and mass of sinful flesh;

That all the Angels and aethereal Powers--

They now, and men hereafter--may discern

From what consummate virtue I have chose

This perfet man, by merit called my Son,

To earn salvation for the sons of men."

So spake the Eternal Father, and all Heaven

Admiring stood a space; then into hymns

Burst forth, and in celestial measures moved, 170 Circling the throne and singing, while the hand

Sung with the voice, and this the argument:--

"Victory and triumph to the Son of God,

Now entering his great duel, not of arms,

But to vanquish by wisdom hellish wiles!

The Father knows the Son; therefore secure

Ventures his filial virtue, though untried,

Against whate'er may tempt, whate'er seduce,

Allure, or terrify, or undermine.

Be frustrate, all ye stratagems of Hell, 180 And, devilish machinations, come to nought!"

So they in Heaven their odes and vigils tuned.

Meanwhile the Son of God, who yet some days

Lodged in Bethabara, where John baptized,

Musing and much revolving in his breast

How best the mighty work he might begin

Of Saviour to mankind, and which way first

Publish his godlike office now mature,

One day forth walked alone, the Spirit leading

And his deep thoughts, the better to converse 190 With solitude, till, far from track of men,

Thought following thought, and step by step led on,

He entered now the bordering Desert wild,

And, with dark shades and rocks environed round,

His holy meditations thus pursued:--

"O what a multitude of thoughts at once

Awakened in me swarm, while I consider

What from within I feel myself, and hear

What from without comes often to my ears,

Ill sorting with my present state compared! 200 When I was yet a child, no childish play

To me was pleasing; all my mind was set

Serious to learn and know, and thence to do,

What might be public good; myself I thought

Born to that end, born to promote all truth,

All righteous things. Therefore, above my years,

The Law of God I read, and found it sweet;

Made it my whole delight, and in it grew

To such perfection that, ere yet my age

Had measured twice six years, at our great Feast 210 I went into the Temple, there to hear

The teachers of our Law, and to propose

What might improve my knowledge or their own,

And was admired by all. Yet this not all

To which my spirit aspired. Victorious deeds

Flamed in my heart, heroic acts--one while

To rescue Israel from the Roman yoke;

Then to subdue and quell, o'er all the earth,

Brute violence and proud tyrannic power,

Till truth were freed, and equity restored: 220 Yet held it more humane, more heavenly, first

By winning words to conquer willing hearts,

And make persuasion do the work of fear;

At least to try, and teach the erring soul,

Not wilfully misdoing, but unware

Misled; the stubborn only to subdue.

These growing thoughts my mother soon perceiving,

By words at times cast forth, inly rejoiced,

And said to me apart, 'High are thy thoughts,

O Son! but nourish them, and let them soar 230 To what highth sacred virtue and true worth

Can raise them, though above example high;

By matchless deeds express thy matchless Sire.

For know, thou art no son of mortal man;

Though men esteem thee low of parentage,

Thy Father is the Eternal King who rules

All Heaven and Earth, Angels and sons of men.

A messenger from God foretold thy birth

Conceived in me a virgin; he foretold

Thou shouldst be great, and sit on David's throne, 240 And of thy kingdom there should be no end.

At thy nativity a glorious quire

Of Angels, in the fields of Bethlehem, sung

To shepherds, watching at their folds by night,

And told them the Messiah now was born,

Where they might see him; and to thee they came,

Directed to the manger where thou lay'st;

For in the inn was left no better room.

A Star, not seen before, in heaven appearing,

Guided the Wise Men thither from the East, 250 To honour thee with incense, myrrh, and gold;

By whose bright course led on they found the place,

Affirming it thy star, new-graven in heaven,

By which they knew thee King of Israel born.

Just Simeon and prophetic Anna, warned

By vision, found thee in the Temple, and spake,

Before the altar and the vested priest,

Like things of thee to all that present stood.'

This having heart, straight I again revolved

The Law and Prophets, searching what was writ 260 Concerning the Messiah, to our scribes

Known partly, and soon found of whom they spake

I am--this chiefly, that my way must lie

Through many a hard assay, even to the death,

Ere I the promised kingdom can attain,

Or work redemption for mankind, whose sins'

Full weight must be transferred upon my head.

Yet, neither thus disheartened or dismayed,

The time prefixed I waited; when behold

The Baptist (of whose birth I oft had heard, 270 Not knew by sight) now come, who was to come

Before Messiah, and his way prepare!

I, as all others, to his baptism came,

Which I believed was from above; but he

Straight knew me, and with loudest voice proclaimed

Me him (for it was shewn him so from Heaven)--

Me him whose harbinger he was; and first

Refused on me his baptism to confer,

As much his greater, and was hardly won.

But, as I rose out of the laving stream, 280 Heaven opened her eternal doors, from whence

The Spirit descended on me like a Dove;

And last, the sum of all, my Father's voice,

Audibly heard from Heaven, pronounced me his,

Me his beloved Son, in whom alone

He was well pleased: by which I knew the time

Now full, that I no more should live obscure,

But openly begin, as best becomes

The authority which I derived from Heaven.

And now by some strong motion I am led 290 Into this wilderness; to what intent

I learn not yet. Perhaps I need not know;

For what concerns my knowledge God reveals."

So spake our Morning Star, then in his rise,

And, looking round, on every side beheld

A pathless desert, dusk with horrid shades.

The way he came, not having marked return,

Was difficult, by human steps untrod;

And he still on was led, but with such thoughts

Accompanied of things past and to come 300 Lodged in his breast as well might recommend

Such solitude before choicest society.

Full forty days he passed--whether on hill

Sometimes, anon in shady vale, each night

Under the covert of some ancient oak

Or cedar to defend him from the dew,

Or harboured in one cave, is not revealed;

Nor tasted human food, nor hunger felt,

Till those days ended; hungered then at last

Among wild beasts. They at his sight grew mild, 310 Nor sleeping him nor waking harmed; his walk

The fiery serpent fled and noxious worm;

The lion and fierce tiger glared aloof.

But now an aged man in rural weeds,

Following, as seemed, the quest of some stray eye,

Or withered sticks to gather, which might serve

Against a winter's day, when winds blow keen,

To warm him wet returned from field at eve,

He saw approach; who first with curious eye

Perused him, then with words thus uttered spake:-- 320 "Sir, what ill chance hath brought thee to this place,

So far from path or road of men, who pass

In troop or caravan? for single none

Durst ever, who returned, and dropt not here

His carcass, pined with hunger and with droughth.

I ask the rather, and the more admire,

For that to me thou seem'st the man whom late

Our new baptizing Prophet at the ford

Of Jordan honoured so, and called thee Son

Of God. I saw and heard, for we sometimes 330 Who dwell this wild, constrained by want, come forth

To town or village nigh (nighest is far),

Where aught we hear, and curious are to hear,

What happens new; fame also finds us out."

To whom the Son of God:--"Who brought me hither

Will bring me hence; no other guide I seek."

"By miracle he may," replied the swain;

"What other way I see not; for we here

Live on tough roots and stubs, to thirst inured

More than the camel, and to drink go far-- 340 Men to much misery and hardship born.

But, if thou be the Son of God, command

That out of these hard stones be made thee bread;

So shalt thou save thyself, and us relieve

With food, whereof we wretched seldom taste."

He ended, and the Son of God replied:--

"Think'st thou such force in bread? Is it not written

(For I discern thee other than thou seem'st),

Man lives not by bread only, but each word

Proceeding from the mouth of God, who fed 350 Our fathers here with manna? In the Mount

Moses was forty days, nor eat nor drank;

And forty days Eliah without food

Wandered this barren waste; the same I now.

Why dost thou, then, suggest to me distrust

Knowing who I am, as I know who thou art?"

Whom thus answered the Arch-Fiend, now undisguised:--

"'Tis true, I am that Spirit unfortunate

Who, leagued with millions more in rash revolt,

Kept not my happy station, but was driven 360 With them from bliss to the bottomless Deep--

Yet to that hideous place not so confined

By rigour unconniving but that oft,

Leaving my dolorous prison, I enjoy

Large liberty to round this globe of Earth,

Or range in the Air; nor from the Heaven of Heavens

Hath he excluded my resort sometimes.

I came, among the Sons of God, when he

Gave up into my hands Uzzean Job,

To prove him, and illustrate his high worth; 370 And, when to all his Angels he proposed

To draw the proud king Ahab into fraud,

That he might fall in Ramoth, they demurring,

I undertook that office, and the tongues

Of all his flattering prophets glibbed with lies

To his destruction, as I had in charge:

For what he bids I do. Though I have lost

Much lustre of my native brightness, lost

To be beloved of God, I have not lost

To love, at least contemplate and admire, 380 What I see excellent in good, or fair,

Or virtuous; I should so have lost all sense.

What can be then less in me than desire

To see thee and approach thee, whom I know

Declared the Son of God, to hear attent

Thy wisdom, and behold thy godlike deeds?

Men generally think me much a foe

To all mankind. Why should I? they to me

Never did wrong or violence. By them

I lost not what I lost; rather by them 390 I gained what I have gained, and with them dwell

Copartner in these regions of the World,

If not disposer--lend them oft my aid,

Oft my advice by presages and signs,

And answers, oracles, portents, and dreams,

Whereby they may direct their future life.

Envy, they say, excites me, thus to gain

Companions of my misery and woe!

At first it may be; but, long since with woe

Nearer acquainted, now I feel by proof 400 That fellowship in pain divides not smart,

Nor lightens aught each man's peculiar load;

Small consolation, then, were Man adjoined.

This wounds me most (what can it less?) that Man,

Man fallen, shall be restored, I never more."

To whom our Saviour sternly thus replied:--

"Deservedly thou griev'st, composed of lies

From the beginning, and in lies wilt end,

Who boast'st release from Hell, and leave to come

Into the Heaven of Heavens. Thou com'st, indeed, 410 As a poor miserable captive thrall

Comes to the place where he before had sat

Among the prime in splendour, now deposed,

Ejected, emptied, gazed, unpitied, shunned,

A spectacle of ruin, or of scorn,

To all the host of Heaven. The happy place

Imparts to thee no happiness, no joy--

Rather inflames thy torment, representing

Lost bliss, to thee no more communicable;

So never more in Hell than when in Heaven. 420 But thou art serviceable to Heaven's King!

Wilt thou impute to obedience what thy fear

Extorts, or pleasure to do ill excites?

What but thy malice moved thee to misdeem

Of righteous Job, then cruelly to afflict him

With all inflictions? but his patience won.

The other service was thy chosen task,

To be a liar in four hundred mouths;

For lying is thy sustenance, thy food.

Yet thou pretend'st to truth! all oracles 430 By thee are given, and what confessed more true

Among the nations? That hath been thy craft,

By mixing somewhat true to vent more lies.

But what have been thy answers? what but dark,

Ambiguous, and with double sense deluding,

Which they who asked have seldom understood,

And, not well understood, as good not known?

Who ever, by consulting at thy shrine,

Returned the wiser, or the more instruct

To fly or follow what concerned him most, 440 And run not sooner to his fatal snare?

For God hath justly given the nations up

To thy delusions; justly, since they fell

Idolatrous. But, when his purpose is

Among them to declare his providence,

To thee not known, whence hast thou then thy truth,

But from him, or his Angels president

In every province, who, themselves disdaining

To approach thy temples, give thee in command

What, to the smallest tittle, thou shalt say 450 To thy adorers? Thou, with trembling fear,

Or like a fawning parasite, obey'st;

Then to thyself ascrib'st the truth foretold.

But this thy glory shall be soon retrenched;

No more shalt thou by oracling abuse

The Gentiles; henceforth oracles are ceased,

And thou no more with pomp and sacrifice

Shalt be enquired at Delphos or elsewhere--

At least in vain, for they shall find thee mute.

God hath now sent his living Oracle 460 Into the world to teach his final will,

And sends his Spirit of Truth henceforth to dwell

In pious hearts, an inward oracle

To all truth requisite for men to know."

So spake our Saviour; but the subtle Fiend,

Though inly stung with anger and disdain,

Dissembled, and this answer smooth returned:--

"Sharply thou hast insisted on rebuke,

And urged me hard with doings which not will,

But misery, hath wrested from me. Where 470 Easily canst thou find one miserable,

And not inforced oft-times to part from truth,

If it may stand him more in stead to lie,

Say and unsay, feign, flatter, or abjure?

But thou art placed above me; thou art Lord;

From thee I can, and must, submiss, endure

Cheek or reproof, and glad to scape so quit.

Hard are the ways of truth, and rough to walk,

Smooth on the tongue discoursed, pleasing to the ear,

And tunable as sylvan pipe or song; 480 What wonder, then, if I delight to hear

Her dictates from thy mouth? most men admire

Virtue who follow not her lore. Permit me

To hear thee when I come (since no man comes),

And talk at least, though I despair to attain.

Thy Father, who is holy, wise, and pure,

Suffers the hypocrite or atheous priest

To tread his sacred courts, and minister

About his altar, handling holy things,

Praying or vowing, and voutsafed his voice 490 To Balaam reprobate, a prophet yet

Inspired: disdain not such access to me."

To whom our Saviour, with unaltered brow:--

"Thy coming hither, though I know thy scope,

I bid not, or forbid. Do as thou find'st

Permission from above; thou canst not more."

He added not; and Satan, bowling low

His gray dissimulation, disappeared,

Into thin air diffused: for now began

Night with her sullen wing to double-shade 500 The desert; fowls in their clay nests were couched;

And now wild beasts came forth the woods to roam.

THE SECOND BOOK

MEANWHILE the new-baptized, who yet remained

At Jordan with the Baptist, and had seen

Him whom they heard so late expressly called

Jesus Messiah, Son of God, declared,

And on that high authority had believed,

And with him talked, and with him lodged--I mean

Andrew and Simon, famous after known,

With others, though in Holy Writ not named--

Now missing him, their joy so lately found,

So lately found and so abruptly gone, 10 Began to doubt, and doubted many days,

And, as the days increased, increased their doubt.

Sometimes they thought he might be only shewn,

And for a time caught up to God, as once

Moses was in the Mount and missing long,

And the great Thisbite, who on fiery wheels

Rode up to Heaven, yet once again to come.

Therefore, as those young prophets then with care

Sought lost Eliah, so in each place these

Nigh to Bethabara--in Jericho 20 The city of palms, AEnon, and Salem old,

Machaerus, and each town or city walled

On this side the broad lake Genezaret,

Or in Peraea--but returned in vain.

Then on the bank of Jordan, by a creek,

Where winds with reeds and osiers whispering play,

Plain fishermen (no greater men them call),

Close in a cottage low together got,

Their unexpected loss and plaints outbreathed:--

"Alas, from what high hope to what relapse 30 Unlooked for are we fallen! Our eyes beheld

Messiah certainly now come, so long

Expected of our fathers; we have heard

His words, his wisdom full of grace and truth.

'Now, now, for sure, deliverance is at hand;

The kingdom shall to Israel be restored:'

Thus we rejoiced, but soon our joy is turned

Into perplexity and new amaze.

For whither is he gone? what accident

Hath rapt him from us? will he now retire 40 After appearance, and again prolong

Our expectation? God of Israel,

Send thy Messiah forth; the time is come.

Behold the kings of the earth, how they oppress

Thy Chosen, to what highth their power unjust

They have exalted, and behind them cast

All fear of Thee; arise, and vindicate

Thy glory; free thy people from their yoke!

But let us wait; thus far He hath performed--

Sent his Anointed, and to us revealed him 50 By his great Prophet pointed at and shown

In public, and with him we have conversed.

Let us be glad of this, and all our fears

Lay on his providence; He will not fail,

Nor will withdraw him now, nor will recall--

Mock us with his blest sight, then snatch him hence:

Soon we shall see our hope, our joy, return."

Thus they out of their plaints new hope resume

To find whom at the first they found unsought.

But to his mother Mary, when she saw 60 Others returned from baptism, not her Son,

Nor left at Jordan tidings of him none,

Within her breast though calm, her breast though pure,

Motherly cares and fears got head, and raised

Some troubled thoughts, which she in sighs thus clad:--

"Oh, what avails me now that honour high,

To have conceived of God, or that salute,

'Hail, highly favoured, among women blest!'

While I to sorrows am no less advanced,

And fears as eminent above the lot 70 Of other women, by the birth I bore:

In such a season born, when scarce a shed

Could be obtained to shelter him or me

From the bleak air? A stable was our warmth,

A manger his; yet soon enforced to fly

Thence into Egypt, till the murderous king

Were dead, who sought his life, and, missing, filled

With infant blood the streets of Bethlehem.

From Egypt home returned, in Nazareth

Hath been our dwelling many years; his life 80 Private, unactive, calm, contemplative,

Little suspicious to any king. But now,

Full grown to man, acknowledged, as I hear,

By John the Baptist, and in public shewn,

Son owned from Heaven by his Father's voice,

I looked for some great change. To honour? no;

But trouble, as old Simeon plain foretold,

That to the fall and rising he should be

Of many in Israel, and to a sign

Spoken against--that through my very soul 90 A sword shall pierce. This is my favoured lot,

My exaltation to afflictions high!

Afflicted I may be, it seems, and blest!

I will not argue that, nor will repine.

But where delays he now? Some great intent

Conceals him. When twelve years he scarce had seen,

I lost him, but so found as well I saw

He could not lose himself, but went about

His Father's business. What he meant I mused--

Since understand; much more his absence now 100 Thus long to some great purpose he obscures.

But I to wait with patience am inured;

My heart hath been a storehouse long of things

And sayings laid up, pretending strange events."

Thus Mary, pondering oft, and oft to mind

Recalling what remarkably had passed

Since first her Salutation heard, with thoughts

Meekly composed awaited the fulfilling:

The while her Son, tracing the desert wild,

Sole, but with holiest meditations fed, 110 Into himself descended, and at once

All his great work to come before him set--

How to begin, how to accomplish best

His end of being on Earth, and mission high.

For Satan, with sly preface to return,

Had left him vacant, and with speed was gone

Up to the middle region of thick air,

Where all his Potentates in council sate.

There, without sign of boast, or sign of joy,

Solicitous and blank, he thus began:-- 120 "Princes, Heaven's ancient Sons, AEthereal Thrones--

Daemonian Spirits now, from the element

Each of his reign allotted, rightlier called

Powers of Fire, Air, Water, and Earth beneath

(So may we hold our place and these mild seats

Without new trouble!)--such an enemy

Is risen to invade us, who no less

Threatens than our expulsion down to Hell.

I, as I undertook, and with the vote

Consenting in full frequence was impowered, 130 Have found him, viewed him, tasted him; but find

Far other labour to be undergone

Than when I dealt with Adam, first of men,

Though Adam by his wife's allurement fell,

However to this Man inferior far--

If he be Man by mother's side, at least

With more than human gifts from Heaven adorned,

Perfections absolute, graces divine,

And amplitude of mind to greatest deeds.

Therefore I am returned, lest confidence 140 Of my success with Eve in Paradise

Deceive ye to persuasion over-sure

Of like succeeding here. I summon all

Rather to be in readiness with hand

Or counsel to assist, lest I, who erst

Thought none my equal, now be overmatched."

So spake the old Serpent, doubting, and from all

With clamour was assured their utmost aid

At his command; when from amidst them rose

Belial, the dissolutest Spirit that fell, 150 The sensualest, and, after Asmodai,

The fleshliest Incubus, and thus advised:--

"Set women in his eye and in his walk,

Among daughters of men the fairest found.

Many are in each region passing fair

As the noon sky, more like to goddesses

Than mortal creatures, graceful and discreet,

Expert in amorous arts, enchanting tongues

Persuasive, virgin majesty with mild

And sweet allayed, yet terrible to approach, 160 Skilled to retire, and in retiring draw

Hearts after them tangled in amorous nets.

Such object hath the power to soften and tame

Severest temper, smooth the rugged'st brow,

Enerve, and with voluptuous hope dissolve,

Draw out with credulous desire, and lead

At will the manliest, resolutest breast,

As the magnetic hardest iron draws.

Women, when nothing else, beguiled the heart

Of wisest Solomon, and made him build, 170 And made him bow, to the gods of his wives."

To whom quick answer Satan thus returned:--

"Belial, in much uneven scale thou weigh'st

All others by thyself. Because of old

Thou thyself doat'st on womankind, admiring

Their shape, their colour, and attractive grace,

None are, thou think'st, but taken with such toys.

Before the Flood, thou, with thy lusty crew,

False titled Sons of God, roaming the Earth,

Cast wanton eyes on the daughters of men, 180 And coupled with them, and begot a race.

Have we not seen, or by relation heard,

In courts and regal chambers how thou lurk'st,

In wood or grove, by mossy fountain-side,

In valley or green meadow, to waylay

Some beauty rare, Calisto, Clymene,

Daphne, or Semele, Antiopa,

Or Amymone, Syrinx, many more

Too long--then lay'st thy scapes on names adored,

Apollo, Neptune, Jupiter, or Pan, 190 Satyr, or Faun, or Silvan? But these haunts

Delight not all. Among the sons of men

How many have with a smile made small account

Of beauty and her lures, easily scorned

All her assaults, on worthier things intent!

Remember that Pellean conqueror,

A youth, how all the beauties of the East

He slightly viewed, and slightly overpassed;

How he surnamed of Africa dismissed,

In his prime youth, the fair Iberian maid. 200 For Solomon, he lived at ease, and, full

Of honour, wealth, high fare, aimed not beyond

Higher design than to enjoy his state;

Thence to the bait of women lay exposed.

But he whom we attempt is wiser far

Than Solomon, of more exalted mind,

Made and set wholly on the accomplishment

Of greatest things. What woman will you find,

Though of this age the wonder and the fame,

On whom his leisure will voutsafe an eye 210 Of fond desire? Or should she, confident,

As sitting queen adored on Beauty's throne,

Descend with all her winning charms begirt

To enamour, as the zone of Venus once

Wrought that effect on Jove (so fables tell),

How would one look from his majestic brow,

Seated as on the top of Virtue's hill,

Discountenance her despised, and put to rout

All her array, her female pride deject,

Or turn to reverent awe! For Beauty stands 220 In the admiration only of weak minds

Led captive; cease to admire, and all her plumes

Fall flat, and shrink into a trivial toy,

At every sudden slighting quite abashed.

Therefore with manlier objects we must try

His constancy--with such as have more shew

Of worth, of honour, glory, and popular praise

(Rocks whereon greatest men have oftest wrecked);

Or that which only seems to satisfy

Lawful desires of nature, not beyond. 230 And now I know he hungers, where no food

Is to be found, in the wide Wilderness:

The rest commit to me; I shall let pass

No advantage, and his strength as oft assay."

He ceased, and heard their grant in loud acclaim;

Then forthwith to him takes a chosen band

Of Spirits likest to himself in guile,

To be at hand and at his beck appear,

If cause were to unfold some active scene

Of various persons, each to know his part; 240 Then to the desert takes with these his flight,

Where still, from shade to shade, the Son of God,

After forty days' fasting, had remained,

Now hungering first, and to himself thus said:--

"Where will this end? Four times ten days I have passed

Wandering this woody maze, and human food

Nor tasted, nor had appetite. That fast

To virtue I impute not, or count part

Of what I suffer here. If nature need not,

Or God support nature without repast, 250 Though needing, what praise is it to endure?

But now I feel I hunger; which declares

Nature hath need of what she asks. Yet God

Can satisfy that need some other way,

Though hunger still remain. So it remain

Without this body's wasting, I content me,

And from the sting of famine fear no harm;

Nor mind it, fed with better thoughts, that feed

Me hungering more to do my Father's will."

It was the hour of night, when thus the Son 260 Communed in silent walk, then laid him down

Under the hospitable covert nigh

Of trees thick interwoven. There he slept,

And dreamed, as appetite is wont to dream,

Of meats and drinks, nature's refreshment sweet.

Him thought he by the brook of Cherith stood,

And saw the ravens with their horny beaks

Food to Elijah bringing even and morn--

Though ravenous, taught to abstain from what they brought;

He saw the Prophet also, how he fled 270 Into the desert, and how there he slept

Under a juniper--then how, awaked,

He found his supper on the coals prepared,

And by the Angel was bid rise and eat,

And eat the second time after repose,

The strength whereof sufficed him forty days:

Sometimes that with Elijah he partook,

Or as a guest with Daniel at his pulse.

Thus wore out night; and now the harald Lark

Left his ground-nest, high towering to descry 280 The Morn's approach, and greet her with his song.

As lightly from his grassy couch up rose

Our Saviour, and found all was but a dream;

Fasting he went to sleep, and fasting waked.

Up to a hill anon his steps he reared,

From whose high top to ken the prospect round,

If cottage were in view, sheep-cote, or herd;

But cottage, herd, or sheep-cote, none he saw--

Only in a bottom saw a pleasant grove,

With chaunt of tuneful birds resounding loud. 290 Thither he bent his way, determined there

To rest at noon, and entered soon the shade

High-roofed, and walks beneath, and alleys brown,

That opened in the midst a woody scene;

Nature's own work it seemed (Nature taught Art),

And, to a superstitious eye, the haunt

Of wood-gods and wood-nymphs. He viewed it round;

When suddenly a man before him stood,

Not rustic as before, but seemlier clad,

As one in city or court or palace bred, 300 And with fair speech these words to him addressed:--

"With granted leave officious I return,

But much more wonder that the Son of God

In this wild solitude so long should bide,

Of all things destitute, and, well I know,

Not without hunger. Others of some note,

As story tells, have trod this wilderness:

The fugitive Bond-woman, with her son,

Outcast Nebaioth, yet found here relief

By a providing Angel; all the race 310 Of Israel here had famished, had not God

Rained from heaven manna; and that Prophet bold,

Native of Thebez, wandering here, was fed

Twice by a voice inviting him to eat.

Of thee those forty days none hath regard,

Forty and more deserted here indeed."

To whom thus Jesus:--"What conclud'st thou hence?

They all had need; I, as thou seest, have none."

"How hast thou hunger then?" Satan replied.

"Tell me, if food were now before thee set, 320 Wouldst thou not eat?" "Thereafter as I like

the giver," answered Jesus. "Why should that

Cause thy refusal?" said the subtle Fiend.

"Hast thou not right to all created things?

Owe not all creatures, by just right, to thee

Duty and service, nor to stay till bid,

But tender all their power? Nor mention I

Meats by the law unclean, or offered first

To idols--those young Daniel could refuse;

Nor proffered by an enemy--though who 330 Would scruple that, with want oppressed? Behold,

Nature ashamed, or, better to express,

Troubled, that thou shouldst hunger, hath purveyed

From all the elements her choicest store,

To treat thee as beseems, and as her Lord

With honour. Only deign to sit and eat."

He spake no dream; for, as his words had end,

Our Saviour, lifting up his eyes, beheld,

In ample space under the broadest shade,

A table richly spread in regal mode, 340 With dishes piled and meats of noblest sort

And savour--beasts of chase, or fowl of game,

In pastry built, or from the spit, or boiled,

Grisamber-steamed; all fish, from sea or shore,

Freshet or purling brook, of shell or fin,

And exquisitest name, for which was drained

Pontus, and Lucrine bay, and Afric coast.

Alas! how simple, to these cates compared,

Was that crude Apple that diverted Eve!

And at a stately sideboard, by the wine, 350 That fragrant smell diffused, in order stood

Tall stripling youths rich-clad, of fairer hue

Than Ganymed or Hylas; distant more,

Under the trees now tripped, now solemn stood,

Nymphs of Diana's train, and Naiades

With fruits and flowers from Amalthea's horn,

And ladies of the Hesperides, that seemed

Fairer than feigned of old, or fabled since

Of faery damsels met in forest wide

By knights of Logres, or of Lyones, 360 Lancelot, or Pelleas, or Pellenore.

And all the while harmonious airs were heard

Of chiming strings or charming pipes; and winds

Of gentlest gale Arabian odours fanned

From their soft wings, and Flora's earliest smells.

Such was the splendour; and the Tempter now

His invitation earnestly renewed:--

"What doubts the Son of God to sit and eat?

These are not fruits forbidden; no interdict

Defends the touching of these viands pure; 370 Their taste no knowledge works, at least of evil,

But life preserves, destroys life's enemy,

Hunger, with sweet restorative delight.

All these are Spirits of air, and woods, and springs,

Thy gentle ministers, who come to pay

Thee homage, and acknowledge thee their Lord.

What doubt'st thou, Son of God? Sit down and eat."

To whom thus Jesus temperately replied:--

"Said'st thou not that to all things I had right?

And who withholds my power that right to use? 380 Shall I receive by gift what of my own,

When and where likes me best, I can command?

I can at will, doubt not, as soon as thou,

Command a table in this wilderness,

And call swift flights of Angels ministrant,

Arrayed in glory, on my cup to attend:

Why shouldst thou, then, obtrude this diligence

In vain, where no acceptance it can find?

And with my hunger what hast thou to do?

Thy pompous delicacies I contemn, 390 And count thy specious gifts no gifts, but guiles."

To whom thus answered Satan, male-content:--

"That I have also power to give thou seest;

If of that power I bring thee voluntary

What I might have bestowed on whom I pleased,

And rather opportunely in this place

Chose to impart to thy apparent need,

Why shouldst thou not accept it? But I see

What I can do or offer is suspect.

Of these things others quickly will dispose, 400 Whose pains have earned
the far-fet spoil." With that

Both table and provision vanished quite,

With sound of harpies' wings and talons heard;

Only the importune Tempter still remained,

And with these words his temptation pursued:--

"By hunger, that each other creature tames,

Thou art not to be harmed, therefore not moved;

Thy temperance, invincible besides,

For no allurement yields to appetite;

And all thy heart is set on high designs, 410 High actions. But wherewith to be achieved?

Great acts require great means of enterprise;

Thou art unknown, unfriended, low of birth,

A carpenter thy father known, thyself

Bred up in poverty and straits at home,

Lost in a desert here and hunger-bit.

Which way, or from what hope, dost thou aspire

To greatness? whence authority deriv'st?

What followers, what retinue canst thou gain,

Or at thy heels the dizzy multitude, 420 Longer than thou canst feed them on thy cost?

Money brings honour, friends, conquest, and realms.

What raised Antipater the Edomite,

And his son Herod placed on Juda's throne,

Thy throne, but gold, that got him puissant friends?

Therefore, if at great things thou wouldst arrive,

Get riches first, get wealth, and treasure heap--

Not difficult, if thou hearken to me.

Riches are mine, fortune is in my hand;

They whom I favour thrive in wealth amain, 430 While virtue, valour, wisdom, sit in want."

To whom thus Jesus patiently replied:--

"Yet wealth without these three is impotent

To gain dominion, or to keep it gained--

Witness those ancient empires of the earth,

In highth of all their flowing wealth dissolved;

But men endued with these have oft attained,

In lowest poverty, to highest deeds--

Gideon, and Jephtha, and the shepherd lad

Whose offspring on the throne of Juda sate 440 So many ages, and shall yet regain

That seat, and reign in Israel without end.

Among the Heathen (for throughout the world

To me is not unknown what hath been done

Worthy of memorial) canst thou not remember

Quintius, Fabricius, Curius, Regulus?

For I esteem those names of men so poor,

Who could do mighty things, and could contemn

Riches, though offered from the hand of kings.

And what in me seems wanting but that I 450 May also in this poverty as soon

Accomplish what they did, perhaps and more?

Extol not riches, then, the toil of fools,

The wise man's cumbrance, if not snare; more apt

To slacken virtue and abate her edge

Than prompt her to do aught may merit praise.

What if with like aversion I reject

Riches and realms! Yet not for that a crown,

Golden in shew, is but a wreath of thorns,

Brings dangers, troubles, cares, and sleepless nights, 460 To him who wears the regal diadem,

When on his shoulders each man's burden lies;

For therein stands the office of a king,

His honour, virtue, merit, and chief praise,

That for the public all this weight he bears.

Yet he who reigns within himself, and rules

Passions, desires, and fears, is more a king--

Which every wise and virtuous man attains;

And who attains not, ill aspires to rule

Cities of men, or headstrong multitudes, 470 Subject himself to anarchy within,

Or lawless passions in him, which he serves.

But to guide nations in the way of truth

By saving doctrine, and from error lead

To know, and, knowing, worship God aright,

Is yet more kingly. This attracts the soul,

Governs the inner man, the nobler part;

That other o'er the body only reigns,

And oft by force--which to a generous mind

So reigning can be no sincere delight. 480 Besides, to give a kingdom hath been thought

Greater and nobler done, and to lay down

Far more magnanimous, than to assume.

Riches are needless, then, both for themselves,

And for thy reason why they should be sought--

To gain a sceptre, oftest better missed."

THE THIRD BOOK

SO spake the Son of God; and Satan stood

A while as mute, confounded what to say,

What to reply, confuted and convinced

Of his weak arguing and fallacious drift;

At length, collecting all his serpent wiles,

With soothing words renewed, him thus accosts:--

"I see thou know'st what is of use to know,

What best to say canst say, to do canst do;

Thy actions to thy words accord; thy words

To thy large heart give utterance due; thy heart 10 Contains of good, wise, just, the perfet shape.

Should kings and nations from thy mouth consult,

Thy counsel would be as the oracle

Urim and Thummim, those oraculous gems

On Aaron's breast, or tongue of Seers old

Infallible; or, wert thou sought to deeds

That might require the array of war, thy skill

Of conduct would be such that all the world

Could not sustain thy prowess, or subsist

In battle, though against thy few in arms. 20 These godlike virtues wherefore dost thou hide?

Affecting private life, or more obscure

In savage wilderness, wherefore deprive

All Earth her wonder at thy acts, thyself

The fame and glory--glory, the reward

That sole excites to high attempts the flame

Of most erected spirits, most tempered pure

AEthereal, who all pleasures else despise,

All treasures and all gain esteem as dross,

And dignities and powers, all but the highest? 30 Thy years are ripe, and over-ripe. The son

Of Macedonian Philip had ere these

Won Asia, and the throne of Cyrus held

At his dispose; young Scipio had brought down

The Carthaginian pride; young Pompey quelled

The Pontic king, and in triumph had rode.

Yet years, and to ripe years judgment mature,

Quench not the thirst of glory, but augment.

Great Julius, whom now all the world admires,

The more he grew in years, the more inflamed 40 With glory, wept that he had lived so long

Ingloroious. But thou yet art not too late."

To whom our Saviour calmly thus replied:--

"Thou neither dost persuade me to seek wealth

For empire's sake, nor empire to affect

For glory's sake, by all thy argument.

For what is glory but the blaze of fame,

The people's praise, if always praise unmixed?

And what the people but a herd confused,

A miscellaneous rabble, who extol 50 Things vulgar, and, well weighed, scarce worth the praise?

They praise and they admire they know not what,

And know not whom, but as one leads the other;

And what delight to be by such extolled,

To live upon their tongues, and be their talk?

Of whom to be dispraised were no small praise--

His lot who dares be singularly good.

The intelligent among them and the wise

Are few, and glory scarce of few is raised.

This is true glory and renown--when God, 60 Looking on the Earth, with approbation marks

The just man, and divulges him through Heaven

To all his Angels, who with true applause

Recount his praises. Thus he did to Job,

When, to extend his fame through Heaven and Earth,

As thou to thy reproach may'st well remember,

He asked thee, 'Hast thou seen my servant Job?'

Famous he was in Heaven; on Earth less known,

Where glory is false glory, attributed

To things not glorious, men not worthy of fame. 70 They err who count it glorious to subdue

By conquest far and wide, to overrun

Large countries, and in field great battles win,

Great cities by assault. What do these worthies

But rob and spoil, burn, slaughter, and enslave

Peaceable nations, neighbouring or remote,

Made captive, yet deserving freedom more

Than those their conquerors, who leave behind

Nothing but ruin wheresoe'er they rove,

And all the flourishing works of peace destroy; 80 Then swell with pride, and must be titled Gods,

Great benefactors of mankind, Deliverers,

Worshipped with temple, priest, and sacrifice?

One is the son of Jove, of Mars the other;

Till conqueror Death discover them scarce men,

Rowling in brutish vices, and deformed,

Violent or shameful death their due reward.

But, if there be in glory aught of good;

It may be means far different be attained,

Without ambition, war, or violence-- 90 By deeds of peace, by wisdom eminent,

By patience, temperance. I mention still

Him whom thy wrongs, with saintly patience borne,

Made famous in a land and times obscure;

Who names not now with honour patient Job?

Poor Socrates, (who next more memorable?)

By what he taught and suffered for so doing,

For truth's sake suffering death unjust, lives now

Equal in fame to proudest conquerors.

Yet, if for fame and glory aught be done, 100 Aught suffered--if young African for fame

His wasted country freed from Punic rage--

The deed becomes unpraised, the man at least,

And loses, though but verbal, his reward.

Shall I seek glory, then, as vain men seek,

Oft not deserved? I seek not mine, but His

Who sent me, and thereby witness whence I am."

To whom the Tempter, murmuring, thus replied:--

"Think not so slight of glory, therein least

Resembling thy great Father. He seeks glory, 110 And for his glory all things made, all things

Orders and governs; nor content in Heaven,

By all his Angels glorified, requires

Glory from men, from all men, good or bad,

Wise or unwise, no difference, no exemption.

Above all sacrifice, or hallowed gift,

Glory he requires, and glory he receives,

Promiscuous from all nations, Jew, or Greek,

Or Barbarous, nor exception hath declared;

From us, his foes pronounced, glory he exacts." 120 To whom our Saviour fervently replied:

"And reason; since his Word all things produced,

Though chiefly not for glory as prime end,

But to shew forth his goodness, and impart

His good communicable to every soul

Freely; of whom what could He less expect

Than glory and benediction--that is, thanks--

The slightest, easiest, readiest recompense

From them who could return him nothing else,

And, not returning that, would likeliest render 130 Contempt instead, dishonour, obloquy?

Hard recompense, unsuitable return

For so much good, so much beneficence!

But why should man seek glory, who of his own

Hath nothing, and to whom nothing belongs

But condemnation, ignominy, and shame--

Who, for so many benefits received,

Turned recreant to God, ingrate and false,

And so of all true good himself despoiled;

Yet, sacrilegious, to himself would take 140 That which to God alone of right belongs?

Yet so much bounty is in God, such grace,

That who advances his glory, not their own,

Them he himself to glory will advance."

So spake the Son of God; and here again

Satan had not to answer, but stood struck

With guilt of his own sin--for he himself,

Insatiable of glory, had lost all;

Yet of another plea bethought him soon:--

"Of glory, as thou wilt," said he, "so deem; 150 Worth or not worth the seeking, let it pass.

But to a Kingdom thou art born--ordained

To sit upon thy father David's throne,

By mother's side thy father, though thy right

Be now in powerful hands, that will not part

Easily from possession won with arms.

Judaea now and all the Promised Land,

Reduced a province under Roman yoke,

Obeys Tiberius, nor is always ruled

With temperate sway: oft have they violated 160 The Temple, oft the Law, with foul affronts,

Abominations rather, as did once

Antiochus. And think'st thou to regain

Thy right by sitting still, or thus retiring?

So did not Machabeus. He indeed

Retired unto the Desert, but with arms;

And o'er a mighty king so oft prevailed

That by strong hand his family obtained,

Though priests, the crown, and David's throne usurped,

With Modin and her suburbs once content. 170 If kingdom move thee not, let move thee zeal

And duty--zeal and duty are not slow,

But on Occasion's forelock watchful wait:

They themselves rather are occasion best--

Zeal of thy Father's house, duty to free

Thy country from her heathen servitude.

So shalt thou best fulfil, best verify,

The Prophets old, who sung thy endless reign--

The happier reign the sooner it begins.

Rein then; what canst thou better do the while?" 180 To whom our Saviour answer thus returned:--

"All things are best fulfilled in their due time;

And time there is for all things, Truth hath said.

If of my reign Prophetic Writ hath told

That it shall never end, so, when begin

The Father in his purpose hath decreed--

He in whose hand all times and seasons rowl.

What if he hath decreed that I shall first

Be tried in humble state, and things adverse,

By tribulations, injuries, insults, 190 Contempts, and scorns, and snares, and violence,

Suffering, abstaining, quietly expecting

Without distrust or doubt, that He may know

What I can suffer, how obey? Who best

Can suffer best can do, best reign who first

Well hath obeyed--just trial ere I merit

My exaltation without change or end.

But what concerns it thee when I begin

My everlasting Kingdom? Why art thou

Solicitous? What moves thy inquisition? 200 Know'st thou not that my rising is thy fall,

And my promotion will be thy destruction?"

To whom the Tempter, inly racked, replied:--

"Let that come when it comes. All hope is lost

Of my reception into grace; what worse?

For where no hope is left is left no fear.

If there be worse, the expectation more

Of worse torments me than the feeling can.

I would be at the worst; worst is my port,

My harbour, and my ultimate repose, 210 The end I would attain, my final good.

My error was my error, and my crime

My crime; whatever, for itself condemned,

And will alike be punished, whether thou

Reign or reign not--though to that gentle brow

Willingly I could fly, and hope thy reign,

From that placid aspect and meek regard,

Rather than aggravate my evil state,

Would stand between me and thy Father's ire

(Whose ire I dread more than the fire of Hell) 220 A shelter and a kind of shading cool

Interposition, as a summer's cloud.

If I, then, to the worst that can be haste,

Why move thy feet so slow to what is best?

Happiest, both to thyself and all the world,

That thou, who worthiest art, shouldst be their King!

Perhaps thou linger'st in deep thoughts detained

Of the enterprise so hazardous and high!

No wonder; for, though in thee be united

What of perfection can in Man be found, 230 Or human nature can receive, consider

Thy life hath yet been private, most part spent

At home, scarce viewed the Galilean towns,

And once a year Jerusalem, few days'

Short sojourn; and what thence couldst thou observe?

The world thou hast not seen, much less her glory,

Empires, and monarchs, and their radiant courts--

Best school of best experience, quickest in sight

In all things that to greatest actions lead.

The wisest, unexperienced, will be ever 240 Timorous, and loth, with novice modesty

(As he who, seeking asses, found a kingdom)

Irresolute, unhardy, unadventrous.

But I will bring thee where thou soon shalt quit

Those rudiments, and see before thine eyes

The monarchies of the Earth, their pomp and state--

Sufficient introduction to inform

Thee, of thyself so apt, in regal arts,

And regal mysteries; that thou may'st know

How best their opposition to withstand." 250 With that (such power was given him then), he took

The Son of God up to a mountain high.

It was a mountain at whose verdant feet

A spacious plain outstretched in circuit wide

Lay pleasant; from his side two rivers flowed,

The one winding, the other straight, and left between

Fair champaign, with less rivers interveined,

Then meeting joined their tribute to the sea.

Fertil of corn the glebe, of oil, and wine;

With herds the pasture thronged, with flocks the hills; 260 Huge cities and high-towered, that well might seem

The seats of mightiest monarchs; and so large

The prospect was that here and there was room

For barren desert, fountainless and dry.

To this high mountain-top the Tempter brought

Our Saviour, and new train of words began:--

"Well have we speeded, and o'er hill and dale,

Forest, and field, and flood, temples and towers,

Cut shorter many a league. Here thou behold'st

Assyria, and her empire's ancient bounds, 270 Araxes and the Caspian lake; thence on

As far as Indus east, Euphrates west,

And oft beyond; to south the Persian bay,

And, inaccessible, the Arabian drouth:

Here, Nineveh, of length within her wall

Several days' journey, built by Ninus old,

Of that first golden monarchy the seat,

And seat of Salmanassar, whose success

Israel in long captivity still mourns;

There Babylon, the wonder of all tongues, 280 As ancient, but rebuilt by him who twice

Judah and all thy father David's house

Led captive, and Jerusalem laid waste,

Till Cyrus set them free; Persepolis,

His city, there thou seest, and Bactra there;

Ecbatana her structure vast there shews,

And Hecatompylos her hunderd gates;

There Susa by Choaspes, amber stream,

The drink of none but kings; of later fame,

Built by Emathian or by Parthian hands, 290 The great Seleucia, Nisibis, and there

Artaxata, Teredon, Ctesiphon,

Turning with easy eye, thou may'st behold.

All these the Parthian (now some ages past

By great Arsaces led, who founded first

That empire) under his dominion holds,

From the luxurious kings of Antioch won.

And just in time thou com'st to have a view

Of his great power; for now the Parthian king

In Ctesiphon hath gathered all his host 300 Against the Scythian, whose incursions wild

Have wasted Sogdiana; to her aid

He marches now in haste. See, though from far,

His thousands, in what martial equipage

They issue forth, steel bows and shafts their arms,

Of equal dread in flight or in pursuit--

All horsemen, in which fight they most excel;

See how in warlike muster they appear,

In rhombs, and wedges, and half-moons, and wings."

He looked, and saw what numbers numberless 310 The city gates
outpoured, light-armed troops

In coats of mail and military pride.

In mail their horses clad, yet fleet and strong,

Prauncing their riders bore, the flower and choice

Of many provinces from bound to bound--

From Arachosia, from Candaor east,

And Margiana, to the Hyrcanian cliffs

Of Caucasus, and dark Iberian dales;

From Atropatia, and the neighbouring plains

Of Adiabene, Media, and the south 320 Of Susiana, to Balsara's haven.

He saw them in their forms of battle ranged,

How quick they wheeled, and flying behind them shot

Sharp sleet of arrowy showers against the face

Of their pursuers, and overcame by flight;

The field all iron cast a gleaming brown.

Nor wanted clouds of foot, nor, on each horn,

Cuirassiers all in steel for standing fight,

Chariots, or elephants indorsed with towers

Of archers; nor of labouring pioners 330 A multitude, with spades and axes armed,

To lay hills plain, fell woods, or valleys fill,

Or where plain was raise hill, or overlay

With bridges rivers proud, as with a yoke:

Mules after these, camels and dromedaries,

And waggons fraught with utensils of war.

Such forces met not, nor so wide a camp,

When Agrican, with all his northern powers,

Besieged Albracea, as romances tell,

The city of Gallaphrone, from thence to win 340 The fairest of her sex, Angelica,

His daughter, sought by many prowest knights,

Both Paynim and the peers of Charlemane.

Such and so numerous was their chivalry;

At sight whereof the Fiend yet more presumed,

And to our Saviour thus his words renewed:--

"That thou may'st know I seek not to engage

Thy virtue, and not every way secure

On no slight grounds thy safety, hear and mark

To what end I have brought thee hither, and shew 350 All this fair sight.
Thy kingdom, though foretold

By Prophet or by Angel, unless thou

Endeavour, as thy father David did,

Thou never shalt obtain: prediction still

In all things, and all men, supposes means;

Without means used, what it predicts revokes.

But say thou wert possessed of David's throne

By free consent of all, none opposite,

Samaritan or Jew; how couldst thou hope

Long to enjoy it quiet and secure 360 Between two such enclosing enemies,

Roman and Parthian? Therefore one of these

Thou must make sure thy own: the Parthian first,

By my advice, as nearer, and of late

Found able by invasion to annoy

Thy country, and captive lead away her kings,

Antigonus and old Hyrcanus, bound,

Maugre the Roman. It shall be my task

To render thee the Parthian at dispose,

Choose which thou wilt, by conquest or by league. 370 By him thou shalt regain, without him not,

That which alone can truly reinstall thee

In David's royal seat, his true successor--

Deliverance of thy brethren, those Ten Tribes

Whose offspring in his territory yet serve

In Habor, and among the Medes dispersed:

The sons of Jacob, two of Joseph, lost

Thus long from Israel, serving, as of old

Their fathers in the land of Egypt served,

This offer sets before thee to deliver. 380 These if from servitude thou shalt restore

To their inheritance, then, nor till then,

Thou on the throne of David in full glory,

From Egypt to Euphrates and beyond,

Shalt reign, and Rome or Caesar not need fear."

To whom our Saviour answered thus, unmoved:--

"Much ostentation vain of fleshly arm

And fragile arms, much instrument of war,

Long in preparing, soon to nothing brought,

Before mine eyes thou hast set, and in my ear 390 Vented much policy, and projects deep

Of enemies, of aids, battles, and leagues,

Plausible to the world, to me worth naught.

Means I must use, thou say'st; prediction else

Will unpredict, and fail me of the throne!

My time, I told thee (and that time for thee

Were better farthest off), is not yet come.

When that comes, think not thou to find me slack

On my part aught endeavouring, or to need

Thy politic maxims, or that cumbersome 400 Luggage of war there shewn me--argument

Of human weakness rather than of strength.

My brethren, as thou call'st them, those Ten Tribes,

I must deliver, if I mean to reign

David's true heir, and his full sceptre sway

To just extent over all Israel's sons!

But whence to thee this zeal? Where was it then

For Israel, or for David, or his throne,

When thou stood'st up his tempter to the pride

Of numbering Israel--which cost the lives 410 of threescore and ten thousand Israelites

By three days' pestilence? Such was thy zeal

To Israel then, the same that now to me.

As for those captive tribes, themselves were they

Who wrought their own captivity, fell off

From God to worship calves, the deities

Of Egypt, Baal next and Ashtaroth,

And all the idolatries of heathen round,

Besides their other worse than heathenish crimes;

Nor in the land of their captivity 420 Humbled themselves, or penitent besought

The God of their forefathers, but so died

Impenitent, and left a race behind

Like to themselves, distinguishable scarce

From Gentiles, but by circumcision vain,

And God with idols in their worship joined.

Should I of these the liberty regard,

Who, freed, as to their ancient patrimony,

Unhumbled, unrepentant, unreformed,

Headlong would follow, and to their gods perhaps 430 Of Bethel and of Dan? No; let them serve

Their enemies who serve idols with God.

Yet He at length, time to himself best known,

Remembering Abraham, by some wondrous call

May bring them back, repentant and sincere,

And at their passing cleave the Assyrian flood,

While to their native land with joy they haste,

As the Red Sea and Jordan once he cleft,

When to the Promised Land their fathers passed.

To his due time and providence I leave them." 440 So spake Israel's true King, and to the Fiend

Made answer meet, that made void all his wiles.

So fares it when with truth falsehood contends.

THE FOURTH BOOK

Perplexed and troubled at his bad success

The Tempter stood, nor had what to reply,

Discovered in his fraud, thrown from his hope

So oft, and the persuasive rhetoric

That sleeked his tongue, and won so much on Eve,

So little here, nay lost. But Eve was Eve;

This far his over-match, who, self-deceived

And rash, beforehand had no better weighed

The strength he was to cope with, or his own.

But--as a man who had been matchless held 10 In cunning, over-reached where least he thought,

To salve his credit, and for very spite,

Still will be tempting him who foils him still,

And never cease, though to his shame the more;

Or as a swarm of flies in vintage-time,

About the wine-press where sweet must is poured,

Beat off, returns as oft with humming sound;

Or surging waves against a solid rock,

Though all to shivers dashed, the assault renew,

(Vain battery!) and in froth or bubbles end-- 20 So Satan, whom repulse upon repulse

Met ever, and to shameful silence brought,

Yet gives not o'er, though desperate of success,

And his vain importunity pursues.

He brought our Saviour to the western side

Of that high mountain, whence he might behold

Another plain, long, but in breadth not wide,

Washed by the southern sea, and on the north

To equal length backed with a ridge of hills

That screened the fruits of the earth and seats of men 30 From cold Septentrion blasts; thence in the midst

Divided by a river, off whose banks

On each side an Imperial City stood,

With towers and temples proudly elevate

On seven small hills, with palaces adorned,

Porches and theatres, baths, aqueducts,

Statues and trophies, and triumphal arcs,

Gardens and groves, presented to his eyes

Above the highth of mountains interposed--

By what strange parallax, or optic skill 40 Of vision, multiplied through air, or glass

Of telescope, were curious to enquire.

And now the Tempter thus his silence broke:--

"The city which thou seest no other deem

Than great and glorious Rome, Queen of the Earth

So far renowned, and with the spoils enriched

Of nations. There the Capitol thou seest,

Above the rest lifting his stately head

On the Tarpeian rock, her citadel

Impregnable; and there Mount Palatine, 50 The imperial palace, compass huge, and high

The structure, skill of noblest architects,

With gilded battlements, conspicuous far,

Turrets, and terraces, and glittering spires.

Many a fair edifice besides, more like

Houses of gods--so well I have disposed

My aerie microscope--thou may'st behold,

Outside and inside both, pillars and roofs

Carved work, the hand of famed artificers

In cedar, marble, ivory, or gold. 60 Thence to the gates cast round thine eye, and see

What conflux issuing forth, or entering in:

Praetors, proconsuls to their provinces

Hasting, or on return, in robes of state;

Lictors and rods, the ensigns of their power;

Legions and cohorts, turms of horse and wings;

Or embassies from regions far remote,

In various habits, on the Appian road,

Or on the AEmilian--some from farthest south,

Syene, and where the shadow both way falls, 70 Meroe, Nilotic isle, and, more to west,

The realm of Bocchus to the Blackmoor sea;

From the Asian kings (and Parthian among these),

From India and the Golden Chersoness,

And utmost Indian isle Taprobane,

Dusk faces with white silken turbants wreathed;

From Gallia, Gades, and the British west;

Germans, and Scythians, and Sarmatians north

Beyond Danubius to the Tauric pool.

All nations now to Rome obedience pay-- 80 To Rome's great Emperor, whose wide domain,

In ample territory, wealth and power,

Civility of manners, arts and arms,

And long renown, thou justly may'st prefer

Before the Parthian. These two thrones except,

The rest are barbarous, and scarce worth the sight,

Shared among petty kings too far removed;

These having shewn thee, I have shewn thee all

The kingdoms of the world, and all their glory.

This Emperor hath no son, and now is old, 90 Old and lascivious, and from Rome retired

To Capreae, an island small but strong

On the Campanian shore, with purpose there

His horrid lusts in private to enjoy;

Committing to a wicked favourite

All public cares, and yet of him suspicious;

Hated of all, and hating. With what ease,

Endued with regal virtues as thou art,

Appearing, and beginning noble deeds,

Might'st thou expel this monster from his throne, 100 Now made a sty, and, in his place ascending,

A victor-people free from servile yoke!

And with my help thou may'st; to me the power

Is given, and by that right I give it thee.

Aim, therefore, at no less than all the world;

Aim at the highest; without the highest attained,

Will be for thee no sitting, or not long,

On David's throne, be prophesied what will."

To whom the Son of God, unmoved, replied:--

"Nor doth this grandeur and majestic shew 110 Of luxury, though called magnificence,

More than of arms before, allure mine eye,

Much less my mind; though thou should'st add to tell

Their sumptuous gluttonies, and gorgeous feasts

On citron tables or Atlantic stone

(For I have also heard, perhaps have read),

Their wines of Setia, Cales, and Falerne,

Chios and Crete, and how they quaff in gold,

Crystal, and myrrhine cups, imbossed with gems

And studs of pearl--to me should'st tell, who thirst 120 And hunger still. Then embassies thou shew'st

From nations far and nigh! What honour that,

But tedious waste of time, to sit and hear

So many hollow compliments and lies,

Outlandish flatteries? Then proceed'st to talk

Of the Emperor, how easily subdued,

How gloriously. I shall, thou say'st, expel

A brutish monster: what if I withal

Expel a Devil who first made him such?

Let his tormentor, Conscience, find him out; 130 For him I was not sent, nor yet to free

That people, victor once, now vile and base,

Deservedly made vassal--who, once just,

Frugal, and mild, and temperate, conquered well,

But govern ill the nations under yoke,

Peeling their provinces, exhausted all

By lust and rapine; first ambitious grown

Of triumph, that insulting vanity;

Then cruel, by their sports to blood inured

Of fighting beasts, and men to beasts exposed; 140 Luxurious by their wealth, and greedier still,

And from the daily Scene effeminate.

What wise and valiant man would seek to free

These, thus degenerate, by themselves enslaved,

Or could of inward slaves make outward free?

Know, therefore, when my season comes to sit

On David's throne, it shall be like a tree

Spreading and overshadowing all the earth,

Or as a stone that shall to pieces dash

All monarchies besides throughout the world; 150 And of my Kingdom there shall be no end.

Means there shall be to this; but what the means

Is not for thee to know, nor me to tell."

To whom the Tempter, impudent, replied:--

"I see all offers made by me how slight

Thou valuest, because offered, and reject'st.

Nothing will please the difficult and nice,

Or nothing more than still to contradict.

On the other side know also thou that I

On what I offer set as high esteem, 160 Nor what I part with mean to give for naught,

All these, which in a moment thou behold'st,

The kingdoms of the world, to thee I give

(For, given to me, I give to whom I please),

No trifle; yet with this reserve, not else--

On this condition, if thou wilt fall down,

And worship me as thy superior Lord

(Easily done), and hold them all of me;

For what can less so great a gift deserve?"

Whom thus our Saviour answered with disdain:-- 170 "I never liked thy talk, thy offers less;

Now both abhor, since thou hast dared to utter

The abominable terms, impious condition.

But I endure the time, till which expired

Thou hast permission on me. It is written,

The first of all commandments, 'Thou shalt worship

The Lord thy God, and only Him shalt serve.'

And dar'st thou to the Son of God propound

To worship thee, accursed? now more accursed

For this attempt, bolder than that on Eve, 180 And more blasphemous; which expect to rue.

The kingdoms of the world to thee were given!

Permitted rather, and by thee usurped;

Other donation none thou canst produce.

If given, by whom but by the King of kings,

God over all supreme? If given to thee,

By thee how fairly is the Giver now

Repaid! But gratitude in thee is lost

Long since. Wert thou so void of fear or shame

As offer them to me, the Son of God-- 190 To me my own, on such abhorred pact,

That I fall down and worship thee as God?

Get thee behind me! Plain thou now appear'st

That Evil One, Satan for ever damned."

To whom the Fiend, with fear abashed, replied:--

"Be not so sore offended, Son of God--

Though Sons of God both Angels are and Men--

If I, to try whether in higher sort

Than these thou bear'st that title, have proposed

What both from Men and Angels I receive, 200 Tetrarchs of Fire, Air, Flood, and on the Earth

Nations besides from all the quartered winds--

God of this World invoked, and World beneath.

Who then thou art, whose coming is foretold

To me most fatal, me it most concerns.

The trial hath indamaged thee no way,

Rather more honour left and more esteem;

Me naught advantaged, missing what I aimed.

Therefore let pass, as they are transitory,

The kingdoms of this world; I shall no more 210 Advise thee; gain them as thou canst, or not.

And thou thyself seem'st otherwise inclined

Than to a worldly crown, addicted more

To contemplation and profound dispute;

As by that early action may be judged,

When, slipping from thy mother's eye, thou went'st

Alone into the Temple, there wast found

Among the gravest Rabbies, disputant

On points and questions fitting Moses' chair,

Teaching, not taught. The childhood shews the man, 220 As morning shews the day. Be famous, then,

By wisdom; as thy empire must extend,

So let extend thy mind o'er all the world

In knowledge; all things in it comprehend.

All knowledge is not couched in Moses' law,

The Pentateuch, or what the Prophets wrote;

The Gentiles also know, and write, and teach

To admiration, led by Nature's light;

And with the Gentiles much thou must converse,

Ruling them by persuasion, as thou mean'st. 230 Without their learning, how wilt thou with them,

Or they with thee, hold conversation meet?

How wilt thou reason with them, how refute

Their idolisms, traditions, paradoxes?

Error by his own arms is best evinced.

Look once more, ere we leave this specular mount,

Westward, much nearer by south-west; behold

Where on the AEgean shore a city stands,

Built nobly, pure the air and light the soil--

Athens, the eye of Greece, mother of arts 240 And Eloquence, native to famous wits

Or hospitable, in her sweet recess,

City or suburban, studious walks and shades.

See there the olive-grove of Academe,

Plato's retirement, where the Attic bird

Trills her thick-warbled notes the summer long;

There, flowery hill, Hymettus, with the sound

Of bees' industrious murmur, oft invites

To studious musing; there Ilissus rowls

His whispering stream. Within the walls then view 250 The schools of ancient sages--his who bred

Great Alexander to subdue the world,

Lyceum there; and painted Stoa next.

There thou shalt hear and learn the secret power

Of harmony, in tones and numbers hit

By voice or hand, and various-measured verse,

AEolian charms and Dorian lyric odes,

And his who gave them breath, but higher sung,

Blind Melesigenes, thence Homer called,

Whose poem Phoebus challenged for his own. 260 Thence what the lofty grave Tragedians taught

In chorus or iambic, teachers best

Of moral prudence, with delight received

In brief sententious precepts, while they treat

Of fate, and chance, and change in human life,

High actions and high passions best describing.

Thence to the famous Orators repair,

Those ancient whose resistless eloquence

Wielded at will that fierce democraty,

Shook the Arsenal, and fulmined over Greece 270 To Macedon and Artaxerxes' throne.

To sage Philosophy next lend thine ear,

From heaven descended to the low-roofed house

Of Socrates--see there his tenement--

Whom, well inspired, the Oracle pronounced

Wisest of men; from whose mouth issued forth

Mellifluous streams, that watered all the schools

Of Academics old and new, with those

Surnamed Peripatetics, and the sect

Epicurean, and the Stoic severe. 280 These here revolve, or, as thou likest, at home,

Till time mature thee to a kingdom's weight;

These rules will render thee a king complete

Within thyself, much more with empire joined."

To whom our Saviour sagely thus replied:--

"Think not but that I know these things; or, think

I know them not, not therefore am I short

Of knowing what I ought. He who receives

Light from above, from the Fountain of Light,

No other doctrine needs, though granted true; 290 But these are false, or little else but dreams,

Conjectures, fancies, built on nothing firm.

The first and wisest of them all professed

To know this only, that he nothing knew;

The next to fabling fell and smooth conceits;

A third sort doubted all things, though plain sense;

Others in virtue placed felicity,

But virtue joined with riches and long life;

In corporal pleasure he, and careless ease;

The Stoic last in philosophic pride, 300 By him called virtue, and his virtuous man,

Wise, perfect in himself, and all possessing,

Equal to God, oft shames not to prefer,

As fearing God nor man, contemning all

Wealth, pleasure, pain or torment, death and life--

Which, when he lists, he leaves, or boasts he can;

For all his tedious talk is but vain boast,

Or subtle shifts conviction to evade.

Alas! what can they teach, and not mislead,

Ignorant of themselves, of God much more, 310 And how the World began, and how Man fell,

Degraded by himself, on grace depending?

Much of the Soul they talk, but all awry;

And in themselves seek virtue; and to themselves

All glory arrogate, to God give none;

Rather accuse him under usual names,

Fortune and Fate, as one regardless quite

Of mortal things. Who, therefore, seeks in these

True wisdom finds her not, or, by delusion

Far worse, her false resemblance only meets, 320 An empty cloud. However, many books,

Wise men have said, are wearisome; who reads

Incessantly, and to his reading brings not

A spirit and judgment equal or superior,

(And what he brings what needs he elsewhere seek?)

Uncertain and unsettled still remains,

Deep-versed in books and shallow in himself,

Crude or intoxicate, collecting toys

And trifles for choice matters, worth a sponge,

As children gathering pebbles on the shore. 330 Or, if I would delight my private hours

With music or with poem, where so soon

As in our native language can I find

That solace? All our Law and Story strewed

With hymns, our Psalms with artful terms inscribed,

Our Hebrew songs and harps, in Babylon

That pleased so well our victor's ear, declare

That rather Greece from us these arts derived--

Ill imitated while they loudest sing

The vices of their deities, and their own, 340 In fable, hymn, or song, so personating

Their gods ridiculous, and themselves past shame.

Remove their swelling epithetes, thick-laid

As varnish on a harlot's cheek, the rest,

Thin-sown with aught of profit or delight,

Will far be found unworthy to compare

With Sion's songs, to all true tastes excelling,

Where God is praised aright and godlike men,

The Holiest of Holies and his Saints

(Such are from God inspired, not such from thee); 350 Unless where moral virtue is expressed

By light of Nature, not in all quite lost.

Their orators thou then extoll'st as those

The top of eloquence--statists indeed,

And lovers of their country, as may seem;

But herein to our Prophets far beneath,

As men divinely taught, and better teaching

The solid rules of civil government,

In their majestic, unaffected style,

Than all the oratory of Greece and Rome. 360 In them is plainest taught, and easiest learnt,

What makes a nation happy, and keeps it so,

What ruins kingdoms, and lays cities flat;

These only, with our Law, best form a king."

So spake the Son of God; but Satan, now

Quite at a loss (for all his darts were spent),

Thus to our Saviour, with stern brow, replied:--

"Since neither wealth nor honour, arms nor arts,

Kingdom nor empire, pleases thee, nor aught

By me proposed in life contemplative 370 Or active, tended on by glory or fame,

What dost thou in this world? The Wilderness

For thee is fittest place: I found thee there,

And thither will return thee. Yet remember

What I foretell thee; soon thou shalt have cause

To wish thou never hadst rejected, thus

Nicely or cautiously, my offered aid,

Which would have set thee in short time with ease

On David's throne, or throne of all the world,

Now at full age, fulness of time, thy season, 380 When prophecies of thee
are best fulfilled.

Now, contrary--if I read aught in heaven,

Or heaven write aught of fate--by what the stars

Voluminous, or single characters

In their conjunction met, give me to spell,

Sorrows and labours, opposition, hate,

Attends thee; scorns, reproaches, injuries,

Violence and stripes, and, lastly, cruel death.

A kingdom they portend thee, but what kingdom,

Real or allegoric, I discern not; 390 Nor when: eternal sure--as without end,

Without beginning; for no date prefixed

Directs me in the starry rubric set."

So saying, he took (for still he knew his power

Not yet expired), and to the Wilderness

Brought back, the Son of God, and left him there,

Feigning to disappear. Darkness now rose,

As daylight sunk, and brought in louring Night,

Her shadowy offspring, unsubstantial both,

Privation mere of light and absent day. 400 Our Saviour, meek, and with untroubled mind

After hisaerie jaunt, though hurried sore,

Hungry and cold, betook him to his rest,

Wherever, under some concourse of shades,

Whose branching arms thick intertwined might shield

From dews and damps of night his sheltered head;

But, sheltered, slept in vain; for at his head

The Tempter watched, and soon with ugly dreams

Disturbed his sleep. And either tropic now

'Gan thunder, and both ends of heaven; the clouds 410 From many a horrid rift abortive poured

Fierce rain with lightning mixed, water with fire,

In ruin reconciled; nor slept the winds

Within their stony caves, but rushed abroad

From the four hinges of the world, and fell

On the vexed wilderness, whose tallest pines,

Though rooted deep as high, and sturdiest oaks,

Bowed their stiff necks, loaden with stormy blasts,

Or torn up sheer. Ill wast thou shrouded then,

O patient Son of God, yet only stood'st 420 Unshaken! Nor yet staid the terror there:

Infernal ghosts and hellish furies round

Environed thee; some howled, some yelled, some shrieked,

Some bent at thee their fiery darts, while thou

Sat'st unappalled in calm and sinless peace.

Thus passed the night so foul, till Morning fair

Came forth with pilgrim steps, in amice grey,

Who with her radiant finger stilled the roar

Of thunder, chased the clouds, and laid the winds,

And griesly spectres, which the Fiend had raised 430 To tempt the Son of God with terrors dire.

And now the sun with more effectual beams

Had cheered the face of earth, and dried the wet

From drooping plant, or dropping tree; the birds,

Who all things now behold more fresh and green,

After a night of storm so ruinous,

Cleared up their choicest notes in bush and spray,

To gratulate the sweet return of morn.

Nor yet, amidst this joy and brightest morn,

Was absent, after all his mischief done, 440 The Prince of Darkness; glad would also seem

Of this fair change, and to our Saviour came;

Yet with no new device (they all were spent),

Rather by this his last affront resolved,

Desperate of better course, to vent his rage

And mad despite to be so oft repelled.

Him walking on a sunny hill he found,

Backed on the north and west by a thick wood;

Out of the wood he starts in wonted shape,

And in a careless mood thus to him said:-- 450 "Fair morning yet betides thee, Son of God,

After a dismal night. I heard the wrack,

As earth and sky would mingle; but myself

Was distant; and these flaws, though mortals fear them,

As dangerous to the pillared frame of Heaven,

Or to the Earth's dark basis underneath,

Are to the main as inconsiderable

And harmless, if not wholesome, as a sneeze

To man's less universe, and soon are gone.

Yet, as being ofttimes noxious where they light 460 On man, beast, plant, wasteful and turbulent,

Like turbulencies in the affairs of men,

Over whose heads they roar, and seem to point,

They oft fore-signify and threaten ill.

This tempest at this desert most was bent;

Of men at thee, for only thou here dwell'st.

Did I not tell thee, if thou didst reject

The perfect season offered with my aid

To win thy destined seat, but wilt prolong

All to the push of fate, pursue thy way 470 Of gaining David's throne no man knows when

(For both the when and how is nowhere told),

Thou shalt be what thou art ordained, no doubt;

For Angels have proclaimed it, but concealing

The time and means? Each act is rightliest done

Not when it must, but when it may be best.

If thou observe not this, be sure to find

What I foretold thee--many a hard assay

Of dangers, and adversities, and pains,

Ere thou of Israel's sceptre get fast hold; 480 Whereof this ominous night that closed thee round,

So many terrors, voices, prodigies,

May warn thee, as a sure foregoing sign."

So talked he, while the Son of God went on,

And staid not, but in brief him answered thus:--

"Me worse than wet thou find'st not; other harm

Those terrors which thou speak'st of did me none.

I never feared they could, though noising loud

And threatening nigh: what they can do as signs

Betokening or ill-boding I contemn 490 As false portents, not sent from God, but thee;

Who, knowing I shall reign past thy preventing,

Obtrud'st thy offered aid, that I, accepting,

At least might seem to hold all power of thee,

Ambitious Spirit! and would'st be thought my God;

And storm'st, refused, thinking to terrify

Me to thy will! Desist (thou art discerned,

And toil'st in vain), nor me in vain molest."

To whom the Fiend, now swoln with rage, replied:--

"Then hear, O Son of David, virgin-born! 500 For Son of God to me is yet in doubt.

Of the Messiah I have heard foretold

By all the Prophets; of thy birth, at length

Announced by Gabriel, with the first I knew,

And of the angelic song in Bethlehem field,

On thy birth-night, that sung thee Saviour born.

From that time seldom have I ceased to eye

Thy infancy, thy childhood, and thy youth,

Thy manhood last, though yet in private bred;

Till, at the ford of Jordan, whither all 510 Flocked to the Baptist, I among the rest

(Though not to be baptized), by voice from Heaven

Heard thee pronounced the Son of God beloved.

Thenceforth I thought thee worth my nearer view

And narrower scrutiny, that I might learn

In what degree or meaning thou art called

The Son of God, which bears no single sense.

The Son of God I also am, or was;

And, if I was, I am; relation stands:

All men are Sons of God; yet thee I thought 520 In some respect far higher so declared.

Therefore I watched thy footsteps from that hour,

And followed thee still on to this waste wild,

Where, by all best conjectures, I collect

Thou art to be my fatal enemy.

Good reason, then, if I beforehand seek

To understand my adversary, who

And what he is; his wisdom, power, intent;

By parle or composition, truce or league,

To win him, or win from him what I can. 530 And opportunity I here have had

To try thee, sift thee, and confess have found thee

Proof against all temptation, as a rock

Of adamant and as a centre, firm

To the utmost of mere man both wise and good,

Not more; for honours, riches, kingdoms, glory,

Have been before contemned, and may again.

Therefore, to know what more thou art than man,

Worth naming the Son of God by voice from Heaven,

Another method I must now begin." 540 So saying, he caught him up, and, without wing

Of hippogrif, bore through the air sublime,

Over the wilderness and o'er the plain,

Till underneath them fair Jerusalem,

The Holy City, lifted high her towers,

And higher yet the glorious Temple reared

Her pile, far off appearing like a mount

Of alablaster, topt with golden spires:

There, on the highest pinnacle, he set

The Son of God, and added thus in scorn:-- 550 "There stand, if thou wilt stand; to stand upright

Will ask thee skill. I to thy Father's house

Have brought thee, and highest placed: highest is best.

Now shew thy progeny; if not to stand,

Cast thyself down. Safely, if Son of God;

For it is written, 'He will give command

Concerning thee to his Angels; in their hands

They shall uplift thee, lest at any time

Thou chance to dash thy foot against a stone.'"

To whom thus Jesus: "Also it is written, 560 'Tempt not the Lord thy God.'" He said, and stood;

But Satan, smitten with amazement, fell.

As when Earth's son, Antaeus (to compare

Small things with greatest), in Irassa strove

With Jove's Alcides, and, oft foiled, still rose,

Receiving from his mother Earth new strength,

Fresh from his fall, and fiercer grapple joined,

Throttled at length in the air expired and fell,

So, after many a foil, the Tempter proud,

Renewing fresh assaults, amidst his pride 570 Fell whence he stood to see his victor fall;

And, as that Theban monster that proposed

Her riddle, and him who solved it not devoured,

That once found out and solved, for grief and spite

Cast herself headlong from the Ismenian steep,

So, strook with dread and anguish, fell the Fiend,

And to his crew, that sat consulting, brought

Joyless triumphals of his hoped success,

Ruin, and desperation, and dismay,

Who durst so proudly tempt the Son of God. 580 So Satan fell; and straight a fiery globe

Of Angels on full sail of wing flew nigh,

Who on their plumy vans received Him soft

From his uneasy station, and upbore,

As on a floating couch, through the blithe air;

Then, in a flowery valley, set him down

On a green bank, and set before him spread

A table of celestial food, divine

Ambrosial fruits fetched from the Tree of Life,

And from the Fount of Life ambrosial drink, 590 That soon refreshed him wearied, and repaired

What hunger, if aught hunger, had impaired,

Or thirst; and, as he fed, Angelic quires

Sung heavenly anthems of his victory

Over temptation and the Tempter proud:--

"True Image of the Father, whether throned

In the bosom of bliss, and light of light

Conceiving, or, remote from Heaven, enshrined

In fleshly tabernacle and human form,

Wandering the wilderness--whatever place, 600 Habit, or state, or motion, still expressing

The Son of God, with Godlike force endued

Against the attempter of thy Father's throne

And thief of Paradise! Him long of old

Thou didst debel, and down from Heaven cast

With all his army; now thou hast avenged

Supplanted Adam, and, by vanquishing

Temptation, hast regained lost Paradise,

And frustrated the conquest fraudulent.

He never more henceforth will dare set foot 610 In paradise to tempt; his snares are broke.

For, though that seat of earthly bliss be failed,

A fairer Paradise is founded now

For Adam and his chosen sons, whom thou,

A Saviour, art come down to reinstall;

Where they shall dwell secure, when time shall be,

Of tempter and temptation without fear.

But thou, Infernal Serpent! shalt not long

Rule in the clouds. Like an autumnal star,

Or lightning, thou shalt fall from Heaven, trod down 620 Under his feet. For proof, ere this thou feel'st

Thy wound (yet not thy last and deadliest wound)

By this repulse received, and hold'st in Hell

No triumph; in all her gates Abaddon rues

Thy bold attempt. Hereafter learn with awe

To dread the Son of God. He, all unarmed,

Shall chase thee, with the terror of his voice,

From thy demoniac holds, possession foul--

Thee and thy legions; yelling they shall fly,

And beg to hide them in a herd of swine, 630 Lest he command them down into the Deep,

Bound, and to torment sent before their time.

Hail, Son of the Most High, heir of both Worlds,

Queller of Satan! On thy glorious work

Now enter, and begin to save Mankind."

Thus they the Son of God, our Saviour meek,

Sung victor, and, from heavenly feast refreshed,

Brought on his way with joy. He, unobserved,

Home to his mother's house private returned.

###

CPSIA information can be obtained
at www.ICGtesting.com
Printed in the USA
LVHW050822300623
751126LV00003B/83